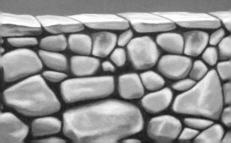

BOUNDARIES

BOUNDARIES

When to Say Yes
When to Say No

To Take Control
of Your Life

by Dr. Henry Cloud
and Dr. John Townsend

ψ
inspirio

RUNNING PRESS
PHILADELPHIA · LONDON

Since the case studies in this book are composites from Dr.
Henry Cloud's and Dr. John Townsend's practices, we have not
attempted to identify which author is counseling which clients.
All names and circumstances have been fictionalized to protect
privacy.

Published in association with Yates & Yates, LLP, Attorneys and
Counselors, Suite 1000, Literary Agent, Orange, CA

Library of Congress Control Number: 2003115611

Running Press ISBN-10: 0-7624-2102-9
Running Press ISBN-13: 978-0-7624-2102-2
Zondervan ISBN 0-310-80759-X

This book may be ordered by mail from the publisher.
Please include $1.00 for postage and handling.
But try your bookstore first!

Running Press Book Publishers
2300 Chestnut Street
Philadelphia, PA 19103-4371

Visit us on the web!
www.runningpress.com
www.inspiriogifts.com

CONTENTS

PART I:
WHAT ARE BOUNDARIES?

1: Boundaries ...10

2: What Does a Boundary Look Like? ... 12

3: Boundary Problems ... 38

4: How Boundaries Are Developed ... 46

5: Ten Laws of Boundaries ... 67

6: Common Boundary Myths ... 75

PART II:
BOUNDARY CONFLICTS

7: Boundaries and Your Family ... 82

8: Boundaries and Your Friends ... 92

9: Boundaries and Your Spouse ... 96

10: Boundaries and Your Children ... 97

11: Boundaries and Work ... 98

12: Boundaries and Your Self ... 108

13: Boundaries and God ... 118

PART III:
DEVELOPING HEALTHY BOUNDARIES

14: Resistance to Boundaries ... 125

15: How to Measure Success

with Boundaries ... 148

PART I:

WHAT ARE
BOUNDARIES?

CHAPTER 1

BOUNDARIES

Confusion about responsibility and ownership in our lives is a problem of *boundaries.* Just as homeowners set physical property lines around their land, we need to set mental, physical, emotional, and spiritual boundaries for our lives to help us distinguish what is our responsibility and what isn't.

Many sincere, dedicated believers struggle with tremendous confusion about when it is biblically appropriate to set limits. This book presents a biblical view of boundaries: what they are, what they protect, how they are developed, how they are injured, how to repair them, and how to use them. Our goal is to help you use biblical boundaries appropriately to achieve the relationships and purposes that God intends for you as his child, and help you see the deeply biblical nature of boundaries as they operate in the character of God, his universe, and his people.

CHAPTER 2

WHAT DOES A BOUNDARY LOOK LIKE?

Invisible Property Lines and Responsibility

Fences, signs, walls, moats with alligators, manicured lawns, or hedges are all physical boundaries. In their differing appearances, they give the same message: THIS IS WHERE MY PROPERTY BEGINS. The owner of the property is legally responsible for what happens on his or her property. Non-owners are not responsible for the property.

In the spiritual world, boundaries are just as real, but often harder to see. Our goal is to help you define your intangible boundaries and recognize them as an everpresent reality that can increase your love and save your life. In reality, these boundaries define your soul, and they help you guard and maintain it (Proverbs 4:23).

Me and Not Me

Boundaries define *what is me* and

what is not me. A boundary shows me where I end and someone else begins, leading me to a sense of ownership. Knowing what I am to own and take responsibility for gives me freedom. However, if I do not "own" my life, my choices and options become very limited.

The Bible tells us clearly what our parameters are and how to protect them, but often our family, or other past relationships, confuses us about our parameters.

In addition to showing us what we are responsible for, boundaries help

us define what is *not* on our property
and what we are *not* responsible for.
We are not, for example, responsible
for other people. Nowhere are we
commanded to have "other-control,"
although we spend a lot of time and
energy trying to get it!

To and For

We are responsible *to* others and
for ourselves. "Carry each other's
burdens," says Galatians 6:2, "and
in this way you will fulfill the law
of Christ." This verse shows our
responsibility *to* one another.

Many times others have "burdens" that are too big to bear. Denying ourselves to do for others what they *cannot* do for themselves is showing the sacrificial love of Christ. This is being responsible "to."

On the other hand, verse 5 says that "each one should carry his own load." Everyone has responsibilities that only he or she can carry. No one can do certain things *for* us.

The Greek word for *burden* means "excess burdens," or burdens that are so heavy that they weigh us down. These burdens are like boulders.

They can crush us. We need help with the boulders—those times of crisis and tragedy in our lives.

In contrast, the Greek word for *load* means "cargo," or "the burden of daily toil." These loads are like knapsacks—we are each expected to carry our own. That means dealing with our own feelings, attitudes, and behaviors, as well as the responsibilities God has given to each one of us, even though it takes effort.

Problems arise when people act as if their "boulders" are daily loads, and refuse help, or as if their "daily loads" are boulders they shouldn't have to carry.

Good In, Bad Out

Boundaries help us keep things that will nurture us inside our fences and keep things that will harm us outside. In short, *boundaries help us keep the good in and the bad out.* They guard our treasures (Matthew 7:6) so that people will not steal them.

Sometimes, we have bad on the inside and good on the outside. In these instances, we need to be able to open up our boundaries to let the good in and the bad out. In other words, our *fences need gates in them.* For example, if I find that I have some pain or sin within, I need to open up and communicate it to God and others, so that I can be healed. Confessing pain and sin helps to "get it out" so that it does not continue to poison me on the inside (1 John 1:9; James 5:16; Mark 7:21–23).

And when the good is on the outside, we need to open our gates and "let it in." Jesus speaks of this phenomenon in "receiving" him and his truth (Revelation 3:20; John 1:12).

Other people have good things to give us, and we need to "open up to them" (2 Corinthians 6:11–13).

God and Boundaries

The concept of boundaries comes from the very nature of God. God defines himself as a distinct, separate being, and he is responsible for himself. He defines and takes responsibility for his personality by telling us what he thinks, feels, plans, allows, will not allow, likes, and dislikes.

He also defines himself as separate from his creation and from us. He tells us who he is and who he is not. For example, he says that he is love and that he is not darkness (1 John 4:16; 1:6).

In addition, he has boundaries within the Trinity. The Father, the Son, and the Spirit are one, but at the same time they are distinct persons with their own boundaries. Each one has his own personhood and responsibilities, as well as a connection and love for one another (John 17:24).

God also limits what he will allow in his yard. He confronts sin and allows consequences for behavior. He guards his house and will not allow evil things to go on there. He invites people in who will love him, and he lets his love flow outward to them at the same time. The "gates" of his boundaries open and close appropriately.

Examples of Boundaries

Words

The most basic boundary-setting word is *no*. It lets others know that you exist apart from them and that

you are in control of you. Being
clear about your no—and your yes—
is a theme that runs throughout the
Bible (Matthew 5:37; James 5:12).

Your words also define your
property for others as you communicate your feelings, intentions, or
dislikes. God does this when he says,
"I like this and I hate that." Or, "I
will do this, and I will not do that."

Truth
Many people live scattered and
tumultuous lives trying to live outside of their own boundaries, not

accepting and expressing the truth of who they are. Honesty about who you are gives you the biblical value of integrity, or oneness.

Geographical Distance

Sometimes physically removing yourself from a situation will help you replenish yourself physically, emotionally, and spiritually after you have given to your limit, as Jesus often did. Or, you can remove yourself to get away from danger and put limits on evil.

Time

Taking time off from a person, or a project, can be a way of regaining ownership over some out-of-control aspect of your life where boundaries need to be set.

Emotional Distance

Emotional distance is a temporary boundary to give your heart the space it needs to be safe; it is never a permanent way of living. People who have been in abusive relationships need to find a safe place to begin to "thaw out" emotionally.

Other People
People subject to another person's addictions, control, or abuse are finding that after years and years of "loving too much," they can find the ability to create boundaries only through a support group. Their support system is giving them the strength to say no to abuse and control for the first time in their lives.

Consequences
Consequences give some good "barbs" to fences. They let people know the seriousness of the trespass

and the seriousness of our respect
for ourselves. This teaches them that
our commitment to living according
to helpful values is something we
hold dear and will fight to protect
and guard.

What's Within My Boundaries?

Feelings
Feelings play an enormous role in
our motivation and behavior. They
should neither be ignored nor placed
in charge. The Bible says to "own"
your feelings and be aware of them.

Attitudes and Beliefs

Attitudes have to do with your orientation toward something, the stance you take toward others, God, life, work, and relationships. Beliefs are anything that you accept as true. We need to *own* our attitudes and convictions because they fall within our property line. We are the ones who feel their effect, *and* the only ones who can change them.

Behaviors

Behaviors have consequences. As Paul says, "A man reaps what he sows" (Galatians 6:7–8). To rescue people from the natural consequences of their behavior is to render them powerless.

Choices

You are the one who makes your choices. You are the one who must live with their consequences. And you are the one who may be keeping yourself from making the choices you could be happy with.

Values

What we value is what we love and assign importance to. When we take responsibility for out-of-control behavior caused by loving the wrong things, or valuing things that have no lasting value, when we confess that we have *a heart that values things that will not satisfy*, we can receive help from God and his people to "create a new heart" within us. Boundaries help us not to deny but to own our old hurtful values so God can change them.

Limits

Two aspects of limits stand out when it comes to creating better boundaries. The first is *setting limits on others.* In reality, setting limits on others is a misnomer. We can't do that. What we *can* do is set limits on our own exposure to people who are behaving poorly; we can't change them or make them behave right.

The other aspect is *setting our own internal limits.* We need to have spaces inside ourselves where we can have a feeling, an impulse, or a desire, without acting it out. *We need self-control without repression.* We need to be able to say no to ourselves. This includes both our destructive desires and some good ones that are not wise to pursue at a given time.

Talents

The parable of the talents says that we are accountable—not to mention much happier—when we are exercising our gifts and being productive. It takes work, practice, learning, prayer, resources, and grace to overcome the fear of failure.

Thoughts

Establishing boundaries in thinking involves three things.

1. We must own our own thoughts. Certainly we should listen to the thoughts of others, but we are also to weigh things for ourselves in the context of relationship, "sharpening" each other as iron, but remaining separate thinkers.

2. We must grow in knowledge and expand our minds. David said of knowing God's Word, "My soul is consumed with longing for your laws at all times. Your statutes are my delight; they are my counselors" (Psalm 119:20, 24). We also learn much about God by studying his creation and his work.

3. We must clarify distorted thinking.
We all have a tendency to not see things clearly, to think and perceive in distorted ways. As we assimilate new information, our thinking adapts and grows closer to reality.

Also we need to make sure that we are communicating our thoughts to others. Paul says, "For who among men knows the thoughts of a man except the man's spirit within him?" (1 Corinthians 2:11). What a great statement about boundaries! We have our own thoughts, and if we want others to know them, we must tell them.

Desires

God loves to give gifts to his children, but he is a wise parent. He wants to make sure his gifts are right for us. To know what to ask for, we have to be in touch with who we really are and what are our real motives.

We are also commanded to play an active role in seeking our desires (Philippians 2:12–13; Ecclesiastes 11:9; Matthew 7:7–11). We need to own our desires and pursue them to find fulfillment in life. "A desire accomplished is sweet to the soul" (Proverbs 13:19 KJV), but it sure is a lot of work!

Love

Our loving heart, like our physical one, *needs an inflow as well as an outflow of lifeblood.* And like its physical counterpart, our heart is a muscle, a trust muscle. This trust muscle needs to be used and exercised; if it is injured it will slow down or weaken.

We need to take responsibility for claiming our hearts as our property and working on our weaknesses so that we can better respond to love. It will open up life to us.

CHAPTER 3

BOUNDARY PROBLEMS

We have categorized the main types of boundary problems, providing you some pegs on which to hang your thoughts.[1]

Compliants: Saying "Yes" to the Bad
When parents teach children that setting boundaries or saying no is bad, they are teaching them that others can do with them as they

wish. They are sending their children defenseless into a world that contains much evil in the form of controlling, manipulative, and exploitative people. Evil in the form of temptations.

This type of boundary conflict is called *compliance*. Compliant people have fuzzy and indistinct boundaries; they "melt" into the demands and needs of other people. They can't stand alone, distinct from people who want something from them. They minimize their differences with others so as not to rock the boat.

The inability to say no to the bad not only keeps us from refusing evil in our lives, *it often keeps us from recognizing evil.* Many compliant people realize too late that they're in a dangerous or abusive relationship.

Avoidants: Saying "No" to the Good

Saying no to the good is a boundary problem called *avoidance*. It's the inability to ask for help, to recognize one's own needs, to let others in. Avoidants withdraw when they are in need; they do not ask for the support of others.

At the heart of the struggle is a confusion of boundaries as walls. Boundaries are supposed to be able to "breathe," to be like fences with a gate that can let the good in and the bad out.

Controllers: Not Respecting Others' Boundaries

The primary problem of individuals *who can't hear no*—which is different from *not being able to say no*—is that they tend to project responsibility for their lives onto others.

Boundary Injuries

Indeed, controllers do lots of damage to others, but they also hurt themselves. Controllers are limited in their ability to take responsibility for owning their lives. Having relied on bullying or indirectness, they can't function on their own in the world. And controllers are isolated. People stay with them out of fear, guilt, or dependency. The only remedy is to let controllers experience the consequences of their irresponsibility.

Nonresponsives:
Not Hearing the Needs of Others

We are responsible to care about and help, *within certain limits*, others whom God places in our lives. To refuse to do so when we have the appropriate resources can be a boundary conflict.

Nonresponsives fall into one of two groups:

1. Those with a critical spirit toward others' needs (a projection of our own hatred of our needs onto others, a problem Jesus addressed in

Matthew 7:1–5). They hate being incomplete in themselves. As a result, they ignore the needs of others.

2. Those who are so absorbed in their own desires and needs they exclude others (a form of narcissism).

Controllers and Nonresponsives
Controlling nonresponsives have a hard time looking past themselves. They see others as responsible for their struggles and are on the look-out for someone to take care of

them. They gravitate toward someone with blurry boundaries, who
will naturally take on too many
responsibilities in the relationship
and who won't complain about it.

CHAPTER 4

HOW BOUNDARIES ARE DEVELOPED

Boundary development is an ongoing process, yet its most crucial stages are in our very early years, where our character is formed. Boundaries also develop in specific, distinct phases that you can perceive. By noting infants and children in their early parental interactions, child development professionals have been able to record the specific phases of boundary development.[2]

Bonding: The Foundation
of Boundary Building

To bond with baby, Mom and Dad need to provide a consistent, warm, loving, and predictable emotional environment for him or her. During this stage, Mom's job is to woo the child into entering a relationship with the world—via attachment with her. (Most often, this is Mom's job, but Dad or a caregiver can do this as well.)

The emotional picture developed by infants forms from thousands of experiences in the first few months of life. The ultimate goal of Mother's "being there" is a state called *emotional object constancy*. Object constancy refers to the child's having an internal sense of belonging and safety, even away from the presence of the mother. All those experiences of constant loving pay off in a child's inner sense of security.

Separation and Individuation: The Construction of a Soul

As infants gain a sense of internal safety and attachment, their need for autonomy, or independence, starts to emerge. Child experts call this *separation and individuation*. "Separation" refers to the child's need to perceive him or herself as distinct from Mother, a "not-me" experience. "Individuation" describes the identity the child develops while separating from Mother. It's a "me" experience.

You can't have "me" until you first have a "not-me." You must first determine who you *aren't* before you discover the true, authentic aspects of your God-given identity.

The separation-individuation process isn't a smooth transition into a person. Three phases are critical to developing healthy boundaries in childhood: hatching, practicing, and rapprochement.

Hatching: "Mommy and Me Aren't the Same"

The first five to ten months of life mark a major shift in infants: from "Mommy and me are the same" to "Mommy and me aren't the same." During this period, babies begin moving out of their passive union with Mother into an active interest in the outside world.

This period is called "hatching" or "differentiation" by child researchers.

It's a time of exploration, of touching, of tasting and feeling new things. Though children in this phase are still dependent on Mother, they aren't wrapped up in closeness with her. The months of nurturing have paid off—the child feels safe enough to start taking risks.

Practicing: "I Can Do Anything!"

During the "practicing" stage, which usually lasts from age ten months to eighteen months (and then returns later), babies learn to walk and begin to use words. While the hatching baby is overwhelmed by this new world and still leans a great deal on Mother, the practicing child is trying to leave her behind! The newfound ability to walk opens up a sense of omnipotence. Toddlers want to try everything, including walking down steep stairs, putting forks into electric sockets, and chasing cats' tails.

In the practicing phase children learn that aggressiveness and taking initiative are good. Parents who firmly and consistently set realistic boundaries with children in this period, but without spoiling their enthusiasm, help them through the transition.

Rapprochement: "I Can't Do Everything"

The *rapprochement* phase is a return to connection with Mother, but this time the child brings a more separate self into the relationship. There are two people now, with differing thoughts and feelings. And the child is ready to relate to the outside world without losing a sense of self.

Let's look at some of the tools toddlers use to build boundaries in this stage.

Anger. Anger is a way for children to know that their experience is different from someone else's. The ability to use anger to distinguish between self and others is a boundary. Children who can appropriately express anger are children who will understand, later in life, when someone is trying to control or hurt them.

Ownership. Being created in God's image, however, means having ownership, or *stewardship*. We are also given stewardship over our time, energy, talents, values, feelings, behavior, money, and so forth. Without a "mine," we have no sense of responsibility to develop, nurture, and protect these resources. Without a "mine," we have no self to give to God and his kingdom.

No: The One-Word Boundary.
Toddlers going through rapprochement frequently use one of the most important words in the human language: the word *no*. It's the first verbal boundary children learn.

The word *no* helps children separate from what they don't like. It gives them the power to make choices. It protects them. It keeps them from feeling completely helpless and powerless.

Parents have two tasks associated with no. First, they need to help their child feel safe enough to say no, thereby *encouraging his or her own boundaries.* Though they certainly can't make all the choices they'd like, young children should be able to have a no that is listened to.

The second task facing parents of children in rapprochement is that of *helping the child respect others' boundaries.* Children need to be able to not only give a no, but also take a no.

Parents need to be able to set and keep age-appropriate boundaries with children, such as time-outs, appropriate confrontations, and spanking, when necessary. "Discipline your son, for in that there is hope; do not be a willing party to his death" (Proverbs 19:18). In other words, help the child learn to take limits before it's too late.

The earlier the child learns good boundaries, the less turmoil he or she experiences later in life. A successful first three years of life will mean a smoother (but not smooth!) adolescence and a better transition into adulthood.

Boundary Injuries:
What Goes Wrong?

Boundary problems are rooted in thousands of encounters with others, as well in our own nature and personality. The most important boundary conflicts, however, occur in the crucial first few years of life. Generally, the earlier and more severe the injury, the deeper the boundary problem.

Withdrawal from Boundaries

Developing children need to know their boundaries will be honored.

It is crucial that their disagreements, their practicing, their experimentation not result in a withdrawal of love.

Please don't misunderstand this. Parental limits are crucial. Children need to know behavioral lines that should not be crossed. They need to suffer biblical, age-appropriate consequences for acting out. What we're talking about here isn't allowing the child free rein. Parents need to stay attached and connected to their children *even when they disagree with them.*

Hostility Against Boundaries

The second boundary injury, easier to spot than the first, is a parent's hostility against boundaries. The parent becomes angry at the child's attempts at separating from him or her. Hostility can emerge in the form of angry words, physical punishment, or inappropriate consequences.

Children need to be under the authority and control of their parents, but when parents punish their child for his growing independence, he will usually retreat into hurt and resentment.

The "my-way-or-else" approach teaches children to pretend to be obedient, at least when the parent is in earshot. The "you-have-a-choice" approach teaches children to be responsible for their own actions.

God's discipline teaches, rather than punishes.

Overcontrol

Overcontrol occurs when otherwise loving parents try to protect their children from making mistakes by having too-strict rules and limits. While a major responsibility of good parents is certainly to control and protect, they must make room for their children to make mistakes. Remember that we learn maturity "by constant use" (Hebrews 5:14).

Overcontrolled children are subject to dependency, enmeshment conflicts, and difficulty setting and keeping firm boundaries. They also have problems taking risks and being creative.

Lack of Limits

No one can really escape the disciplines of life. They will always win out. We always reap what we sow. And the later in life it is, the sadder a picture it is, for the stakes are higher.

Inconsistent Limits

Sometimes, due to their confusion about rearing children or their own injuries, some parents combine strict and lax limits, sending conflicting messages to children. The children don't know what the rules of family and life are.

Trauma

A trauma is an intensely painful

emotional experience, rather than a character pattern. Emotional, physical, and sexual abuse are traumatic. Accidents and debilitating illnesses are traumatic. Severe losses such as the death of a parent, divorce, or extreme financial hardship are also traumatic.

A trauma can affect boundary development because it shakes up two necessary foundations to children's growth:

1. The world is reasonably safe.

2. They have control over their lives.

Our Own Character Traits

We contribute to our boundary issues by our own individual character styles. For example, some people with a constitutionally greater amount of aggression deal with boundary problems more confrontationally. And some with less aggression shy more from boundaries.

Our Own Sinfulness

Depravity is what we inherited from Adam and Eve. It is our resistance to being creatures under God, our resistance to humility. It's a refusal to accept our position, and a lust for being omnipotent and "in charge," not needing anyone and not accountable to anyone. Our depravity enslaves us to the law of sin and death, from which only Christ can save us (Romans 8:2).

CHAPTER 5

TEN LAWS OF BOUNDARIES

Law #1: The Law of Sowing and Reaping

The law of cause and effect is a basic law of life. The Bible calls it the Law of Sowing and Reaping. "You reap whatever you sow. If you sow to your own flesh, you will reap corruption from the flesh; but if you sow to the Spirit, you will reap eternal life from the Spirit" (Galatians 6:7–8 NRSV).

Law #2: The Law of Responsibility

The Law of Responsibility includes loving others. Problems arise when boundaries of responsibility are confused. We are to *love* one another, not *be* one another. You are responsible for *yourself*. I am responsible for *myself*.

Law #3: The Law of Power

What *do* I have the power to do?

1. You have the power to agree with the truth about your problems.
2. You have the power to submit your inability to God.

3. You have the power to search and ask God and others to reveal more and more about what is within your boundaries.
4. You have the power to turn from the evil that you find within you.
5. You have the power to humble yourself and ask God and others to help you with your developmental injuries and leftover childhood needs.
6. You have the power to seek out those that you have injured and make amends.

Law #4: The Law of Respect

If we love and respect people who tell us no, they will love and respect our no. Freedom begets freedom. If we are walking in the Spirit, we give people the freedom to make their own choices. "Where the Spirit of the Lord is, there is freedom" (2 Corinthians 3:17).

Law #5: The Law of Motivation

The Law of Motivation says this: Freedom first, service second. If you serve to get free of your fear, you are doomed to failure. Let God work on the fears, resolve them, and create some healthy boundaries to guard the freedom you were called to.

Law #6: The Law of Evaluation

You need to evaluate the effects of setting boundaries and be responsible to the other person, but that does not mean you should avoid setting boundaries because someone responds with hurt or anger. We need to see how this hurt is helpful to others and sometimes the best thing that we can do for them and the relationship.

Law #7: The Law of Proactivity

This is the beginning of the establishment of *proactive*, instead of reactive, boundaries, where you are able to use the freedom you gained through reacting to love, enjoy, and serve one another. Proactive people show you what they love, what they want, what they purpose, and what they stand for, rather than what they hate, what they don't like, what they stand against, and what they will not do.

Law #8: The Law of Envy

The problem with envy is that it focuses outside our boundaries, onto others. Your envy should always be a sign to you that you are lacking something. At that moment, you should ask God to help you understand what you resent, why you do not have whatever you are envying, and whether you truly desire it.

Law #9: The Law of Activity

Many times we have boundary problems because we lack initiative— the God-given ability to propel ourselves into life. Passivity never pays off. God wants us to be assertive and active, seeking and knocking on the door of life.

Law #10: The Law of Exposure

A boundary is a property line. It defines where you begin and end. The Law of Exposure says that your boundaries need to be made visible to others and communicated to them in relationship.

CHAPTER 6

COMMON
BOUNDARY MYTHS

MYTH #1: If I Set
Boundaries, I'm Being Selfish

Our lives are our responsibility. We
are to develop our abilities, feelings,
thoughts, and behaviors. Our spiritual and emotional growth is God's
"interest" on his investment in us.
When we say no to people and activ-
ities that are hurtful to us, we are
protecting God's investment.

MYTH #2: Boundaries
Are a Sign of Disobedience

Having a "no" helps us to clarify, to be honest, to tell the truth about our motives; then we can allow God to work in us.

MYTH #3: If I Begin Setting
Boundaries, I Will Be Hurt by Others

Those who can't respect our boundaries are telling us that they don't love our no. They only love our yes, our compliance. Better to learn about their character and take steps to fix the problem than never to know.

MYTH #4: If I Set Boundaries, I Will Hurt Others

Appropriate boundaries don't control, attack, or hurt anyone. They simply prevent your treasures from being taken at the wrong time. Saying no to adults, who are responsible for getting their own needs met, may cause some discomfort. But it doesn't cause injury.

MYTH #5: Boundaries Mean That I Am Angry

Remember the "early warning system" function of anger. We feel it when we are violated. If you can prevent boundary violation in the first place, you don't need the anger. You are more in control of your life and values.

MYTH #6: When Others Set Boundaries, It Injures Me

It is helpful to remember Jesus' Golden Rule here: "In everything, do to others what you would have them do to you" (Matthew 7:12). Apply it to setting limits. Do you want others to respect your boundaries? Then you must be willing to respect theirs.

MYTH #7: Boundaries Cause Feelings of Guilt

The idea is that *because we have received something, we owe something.* The problem is the nonexistent debt. The love we receive, or money, or time—or anything which causes us to feel obligated—should be accepted as a gift. "Gift" implies no strings attached. All that's really needed is gratitude.

MYTH #8: Boundaries Are Permanent, and I'm Afraid of Burning My Bridges

It's important to understand that your no is always subject to you. You own your boundaries. If someone responds maturely and lovingly, you can renegotiate the boundary. In addition, you can change the boundary if you are in a safer place.

PART II:

BOUNDARY CONFLICTS

CHAPTER 7

BOUNDARIES AND YOUR FAMILY

People who own their lives do not feel guilty when they make choices about where they are going. They take other people into consideration, but when they make choices for the wishes of others, they are choosing out of love, not guilt; to advance a good, not to avoid being bad.

Signs of a Lack of Boundaries

Catching the Virus
When your relationship with one
person has the power to affect your
relationships with others, you are
giving one person way too much
power in your life.

Second Fiddle
Many marriages fail because one
partner fails to set clear boundaries
with the family of origin, and the
spouse and children get leftovers.

May I Have My Allowance, Please?

An adult who does not stand on his own financially is still a child. To be an adult, you must live within your means and pay for your own failures.

Mom, Where Are My Socks?

A person may be financially on his own, but allows his family of origin to perform certain life management functions. On the surface these things do not appear to be serious problems. But often, Mom and Dad are symbolically keeping their adult child from emotionally leaving home.

Three's a Crowd
Triangulation is the failure to resolve a conflict between two persons and the pulling in of a third to take sides. The third person has no business in the conflict, but *is used for comfort and validation by the ones who are afraid to confront each other.*

Who's the Child Here, Anyhow?
Some people have parents who are stuck in childish patterns of irresponsibility. When they became adults,

they had a difficult time setting boundaries between themselves and their irresponsible parents. Good boundaries prevent resentment.

But I'm Your Brother

An irresponsible adult child depends on a responsible adult sibling to avoid growing up and leaving the family. (We are not talking about a true needy sibling who has a mental or physical impairment.) The irresponsible child continues to play old family games well into adulthood.

Resolution of Boundary Problems with Family

Establishing boundaries with families of origin is a tough task, but one with great reward. It is a process, with certain distinguishable steps.

Identify the Symptom
Look at your own life situation and see where boundary problems exist with your parents and siblings.

Identify the Conflict
Discover what dynamic is being played out. For example, what "law

of boundaries" are you violating?

Identify the Need That Drives the Conflict

You do not act in inappropriate ways for no reason. You are often trying to meet some underlying need that your family of origin did not meet. You must face this deficit and accept that it can only be met in your new family of God.

Take in and Receive the Good

It is not enough to understand your need. *You must get it met.* God is will-

ing to meet your needs through his
people, but you must humble yourself, reach out to a good support system, and take in the good.

Practice Boundary Skills
Your boundary skills are fragile and
new. You can't take them immediately
into a difficult situation. Practice
them in situations where they will be
honored and respected.

Say No to the Bad
When you are in the beginning
stages of recovery, you need to avoid

people who have abused and controlled you in the past.

Forgive the Aggressor

When you refuse to forgive someone,
you still want something from that
person, and even if it is revenge that
you want, it *keeps you tied to him forever.*

Respond, Don't React

If someone is able to cause havoc
by doing or saying something, she
is in control of you at that point,
and your boundaries are lost. When
you *respond*, you remain in control,

with options and choices.

Learn to Love in Freedom and Responsibility, Not in Guilt

The person who has to remain forever in a protective mode is losing
out on love and freedom. Boundaries
in no way mean to stop loving. They
mean the opposite: you are gaining
freedom to love.

CHAPTER 8

BOUNDARIES AND YOUR FRIENDS

Let's define friendship as *a nonromantic relationship that is attachment-based rather than function-based.*

Questions about Friendship Boundary Conflicts

Question #1: Aren't Friendships Easily Broken?

It's scary to realize that the only thing holding our friends to us is love. And that's the one thing we can't control. However, as we enter more and more into an attachment-based life, we learn that the bonds of a true friendship are not easily broken. In a good relationship, we can set limits that will strengthen, not injure, the connection.

Question #2: How Can I Set Boundaries in Romantic Friendships?

It's best to learn the skill of setting boundaries in nonromantic arenas, where the attachments and commitments are greater. Once we've learned to recognize, set, and keep our biblical boundaries, we can use them on the adult playground called dating.

Question #3: What If My Closest Friends Are My Family?

If you have never questioned, set boundaries, or experienced conflict with your family members, you may not have an adult-to-adult connection with your family. If you have no other "best friends" than your family, you need to take a close look at those relationships. You may be afraid of becoming an autonomous adult.

Question #4: How Can I Set Limits with Needy Friends?

When the Bible tells us to comfort with the comfort with which we are comforted (2 Corinthians 1:4), it's telling us that we need to be comforted before we can comfort. That may mean setting boundaries on our ministries so that we can be nurtured by our friends. We must distinguish between the two.

CHAPTER 9

BOUNDARIES AND YOUR SPOUSE

In a marriage, as in no other relationship, the need for revealing your boundaries is important. Passive boundaries, such as withdrawal, triangulation, pouting, affairs, and passive-aggressive behavior, are extremely destructive to a relationship. Boundaries need to be communicated first verbally and then with actions. They need to be clear and unapologetic.

CHAPTER 10

BOUNDARIES AND YOUR CHILDREN

Parents have a sober responsibility: teaching their children to have an internal sense of boundaries and to respect the boundaries of others.

Developing boundaries in young children is that proverbial ounce of prevention. If we teach responsibility, limit setting, and delay of gratification early on, the smoother our children's later years of life will be.

CHAPTER 11

BOUNDARIES AND WORK

Work and Character Development

The New Testament teaches that jobs offer more than temporal fulfillment and rewards on earth. Work is the place to develop our character in preparation for the work we will do forever.

Problems in the Workplace

If people took responsibility for their own work and set clear limits, most of the problems in the workplace would not exist.

Problem #1: Getting Saddled with Another Person's Responsibilities

Favors and sacrifices are part of the Christian life. Enabling is not. Learn to tell the difference by seeing if your giving is helping the other person to become better or worse.

Problem #2: Working Too Much Overtime

You need to take responsibility for yourself and take steps to change your situation. Here are some suggested steps that will help:

1. Set boundaries on your work.
Decide how much overtime you are willing to do. Some overtime during seasonal crunches may be expected of you.

2. Review your job description, if one exists.

3. Make a list of the tasks you need to complete in the next month.
Make a copy of the list and assign your own priority to each item.

Indicate on this copy any tasks that are not part of your job description.

4. Make an appointment to see your boss to discuss your job overload. Together you should review the list of tasks you need to complete in the next month. Have your boss prioritize the tasks.

Problem #3: Misplaced Priorities Know what you can do and when you can do it, and say no to everything else. Learn to know your limits and enforce them.

Problem #4: Difficult Co-workers

To see another person as the problem to be fixed is to give that person power over you and your well-being. Because you cannot change another person, you are out of control. *You* are the one in pain, and only *you* have the power to fix it.

Problem #5: Critical Attitudes

Avoid trying to gain the approval of a supercritical person. It will never work, and you will only feel controlled. And avoid getting in arguments and discussions. You will

never win. Stay separate. Keep your
boundaries. Don't get sucked into
their game.

Problem #6: Conflicts with Authority

"Transference" is when you experience feelings in the present that really
belong to some unfinished business in
the past. It happens frequently with
bosses because they are authority
figures. Until you face your own
feelings, you can't even see who others really are. You are looking at
them through your own distortions,
through your own unfinished busi-

ness. When you see others clearly without transference, you will know how to deal with them.

Problem #7: Expecting Too Much of Work

The workplace ideally should be supportive, safe, and nurturing. But this atmosphere should primarily support the employee in work-related ways—to help her learn, improve, and get a job done. The problem arises when someone wants the job to provide what her parents did not provide for her: primary nurturing, relationship, self-esteem, and approval.

Problem #8: Taking Work-Related Stress Home

We need to have good boundaries on work and keep it out of the home. Conflicts at work need to be dealt with and worked through so they do not begin to affect the rest of your life. And care should be taken that the job, which is literally never done, does not continue to spill over into personal life and cost you relationships and other things that matter.

Problem #9: Disliking Your Job

Many people are unable to ever find a true work identity. They have not been able to own their own gifts, talents, wants, desires, and dreams because they are unable to set boundaries on others' definitions and expectations of them. You must make sure that your boundaries are strong enough that you do not let others define you. Instead, work with God to find out who you really are and what kind of work you are made for.

Finding Your Life's Work

As you develop your talents, look at your work as a partnership between you and God. He has given you gifts, and he wants you to develop them. Commit your way to the Lord, and you will find your work identity. Ask him to help.

CHAPTER 12

BOUNDARIES AND YOUR SELF

Our Out-of-Control Soul

Eating

For overeaters, food serves as a false boundary. They might use food to avoid intimacy by gaining weight and becoming less attractive. Or they might binge as a way to get false closeness. For bingers, the "comfort" from food is less scary than the prospect of real relationships, where boundaries would be necessary.

Money

When we have difficulty saying no to spending more than we should, we run the risk of becoming someone else's servant: "The rich rule over the poor, and the borrower is servant to the lender" (Proverbs 22:7).

Time

Undeveloped time self-boundaries often stem from one or more of the following causes:

1. Omnipotence. These people have unrealistic, somewhat grandiose expectations of what they can accomplish in a given amount of time.

2. Overresponsibility for the feelings of others. They think that leaving a party too early will cause the host to feel abandoned.

3. Lack of realistic anxiety. They live so much in the present that they neglect to plan ahead for traffic, parking the car, or dressing for an outing.

4. Rationalization. They minimize the distress and inconvenience that others must put up with because of their lateness.

Task Completion

The problem with many poor finishers lies in one of the following causes:

1. Resistance to structure. Poor finishers feel that submitting to the discipline of a plan is a putdown.

2. Fear of success. Poor finishers are overconcerned that success will cause others to envy and criticize them.

3. Lack of follow-through. Poor finishers have an aversion to the boring "nuts and bolts" of turning the crank on a project.

4. Distractibility. Poor finishers are unable to focus on a project until it's done. They have often never developed competent concentration skills.

5. Inability to delay gratification. Poor finishers are unable to work through the pain of a project to experience the satifaction of a job well done.

6. Inability to say no to other pressures. Poor finishers are unable to say no to other people and projects. They don't have time to finish any job well.

The Tongue

When we can't set boundaries on what comes from our lips, our words are in charge—not us. But we are still responsible for those words. "But I tell you that men will have to give account on the day of judgment for every careless word they have spoken" (Matthew 12:36).

Sexuality

As in most internal boundary conflicts, sexual boundarylessness becomes a tyrant, demanding and insatiable. No matter how many orgasms are reached, the desire only deepens, and the inability to say no to one's lusts drives one deeper into despair and hopelessness.

Alcohol and Substance Abuse

Divorce, job loss, financial havoc, medical problems, and death are the fruits of the inability to set limits in regard to alcohol and drug dependencies.

Why Doesn't My "No" Work?

1. We are our own worst enemies.
Previously, we were only responsible
to, not for, the other party. Now we
have a great deal more involvement—
we *are* the other party. We *are*
responsible for ourselves.

**2. We withdraw from relationship
when we most need it.** Grace must
come from the outside of ourselves
to be useful and healing.

3. We try to use willpower to solve our boundary problems. If we depend on willpower alone, we are denying the power of the relationship promised in the cross. The truth is, willpower alone is useless against self-boundary struggles:

Establishing Boundaries with Yourself

The five-point formula for developing self-boundaries is cyclical. That is, as you deal with real needs, fail, get empathic feedback, suffer consequences, and are restored, you build stronger internal boundaries each time. As you stay with your goal and with the right people, you will build a sense of self-restraint that can truly become part of your character for life.

If You Are a Victim

In many cases the severe nature of the need is such that the victim will be unable to set boundaries without professional help. We strongly urge abuse victims to seek out a counselor who can guide them in establishing and maintaining appropriate boundaries.

CHAPTER 13

BOUNDARIES AND GOD

Respecting Boundaries

God has designed the world so
that boundaries are to be respected.
He respects ours, and we need to
respect his.

God respects our boundaries in
many ways. First, *he leaves work for us
to do that only we can do.* And he
allows us to experience the painful
consequences of our behavior so that
we will change. Second, *he respects our*

118

no. He tries neither to control nor nag us. He allows us to say no and go our way. He respects boundaries.

Anger

In our deeper honesty and ownership of our true person, there is room for expressing anger at God. He wants to hear it all, no matter how bad it seems to us. When we own what is within our boundaries, when we bring it into the light, God can transform it with his love.

Respecting His Boundaries

God is free from us. When he does something for us, he does it out of choice. We can rest in his pure love; he has no hidden resentment in what he does. His freedom allows him to love.

In the same way that we want others to respect our no, God wants us to respect his. We do not like others trying to manipulate or control us with guilt, and neither does he.

"I Respectfully Disagree"

God doesn't want us to withdraw our love when he says no. But he has nothing at all against our trying to persuade him to change his mind. In fact, he asks for us to be tenacious. Often he says, "Wait," seeing how much we really want something. Other times, it seems he changes his mind as a result of our relationship with him.

Respecting His Own

God is a good model. When we are hurting, we need to take responsibility for the hurt and make some appropriate moves to make things better. This may mean letting go of someone and finding new friends. It may mean forgiving someone and letting them off the hook so we can feel better.

A Real Relationship

Boundaries are inherent in any relationship God has created, for they define the two parties who are loving each other. They let us see God as he really is. They enable us to negotiate life, fulfilling our responsibilities and requirements. If we are trying to do his work for him, we will fail. If we are wishing for him to do our work for us, he will refuse. But if we do our work, and God does his, we will find strength in a real relationship with our Creator.

PART III:

DEVELOPING
HEALTHY BOUNDARIES

CHAPTER 14

RESISTANCE TO BOUNDARIES

Even with the desire for a better life, we can be reluctant to do the work of boundaries because it will be a war. The battles fall into two categories: outside resistance and inside resistance—the resistance we get from others and the resistance we get from ourselves.

Outside Resistance

Anger: If you keep your boundaries, those who are angry at you will have to learn self-control for the first time, instead of "other control," which has been destructive to them anyway. When they no longer have control over you, they will find a different way to relate.

Guilt: Some people will try to make you feel bad about deciding how you will spend your own time or resources, about growing up and separating from your parents, or about having a life separate from a friend or spiritual leader. Empathize with the distress people are feeling, but make it clear that it is *their* distress.

Consequences and Countermoves

You face a risk in setting boundaries and gaining control of your life. In most instances, the results are not drastic, for as soon as the other person finds out that you are serious, they start to change. They find the limit setting to be something good for them.

Physical Resistance

Often people who try to set limits are physically abused. If you are in this situation, find other people to help you set limits on the abuse. Find a counselor, arrange to call people in your church if violence erupts, arrange for a place to stay overnight if you are threatened, no matter what the hour. Call the police and an attorney. Get a restraining order on such an individual if he will respect no other limit. Do it for yourself and for your children.

Pain of Others

When we begin to set boundaries with people we love, a really hard thing happens: they hurt. They may feel a hole where you used to plug up their aloneness, their disorganization, or their financial irresponsibility. Whatever it is, they will feel a loss.

If you love them, this will be difficult for you to watch. But, when you are dealing with someone who is hurting, remember that your boundaries are both necessary for you and helpful for them. If you have been enabling them to be irresponsible,

your limit setting may nudge them
toward responsibility.

Blamers

Blamers will act as though your saying
no is killing them, and they will react
with a "How could you do this to
me?" message. They are likely to cry,
pout, or get angry. Remember that
blamers have a character problem. If
they make it sound as though their
misery is because of your not giving
something to them, they are blaming
and demanding what is yours.

Real Needs

You may need to set boundaries on people in real need. If you are a loving person, it will break your heart to say no to someone you love who is in need. But there are limits to what you can and can't give; you need to say no appropriately.

Forgiveness and Reconciliation

The Bible is clear about two principles: (1) We always need to forgive, but (2) we don't always achieve reconciliation. Forgiveness is something that we do in our hearts; we release someone from a debt that they owe us. Reconciliation is another matter. God forgave the world, but the whole world is not reconciled to him. Forgiveness takes one; reconciliation takes two.

Internal Resistances

Let's look at boundaries in regard to our internal resistance to growth.

Human Need

When we have unmet needs, we need to take inventory of these broken places inside and begin to have those needs met in the body of Christ so that we will be strong enough to fight the boundary fights of adult life.

Unresolved Grief and Loss

Grief has to do with letting go of the "bad." Many times when someone is unable to set boundaries, it is because they cannot let go of the person with whom they are fused.

You will be amazed how much can change in your life when you finally begin to let go of what you can never have. Letting go is the way to serenity. Grief is the path.

Internal Fears of Anger

If angry people can make you lose
your boundaries, you probably have
an angry person in your head that you
still fear. You will need to work
through some of the hurt you experienced in that angry past. You need
love to allow you to let go of that
angry person and stand up to the
adults you now face.

Here are the steps you need to take:

1. Realize it is a problem.

2. Go talk to someone about your paralysis. You will not work this out alone.

3. In your support relationships, find the source of your fear and begin to recognize the person in your head that the angry person represents.

4. Talk out your hurts and feelings regarding these past issues.

5. Practice the boundary-setting skills in this book.

6. Don't go into automatic pilot and give up your boundaries either by fighting or by being passive. Give yourself time and space until you can respond.

7. When you are ready, respond. Stick to your decisions. Just reiterate what you will do or not do, and let them be angry. Tell them that you care for them; maybe ask if you can do anything else to help. But your no still stands.

8. Regroup. Talk to your support people about the interaction and see if you kept your ground, lost ground, or were attacking.

9. Keep practicing. Role play, continue to gain insight and understanding about the past, and grieve your losses. Continue to gain skills in the present.

Fear of the Unknown

Another powerful internal resistance is the fear of the unknown. Here are some ideas that may prove helpful:

1. Pray. No better antidote to anxiety about the future exists than faith, hope, and the realization of the one who loves us.

2. Read the Bible. God continually tells us in the Bible that he has our future in his hands and that he promises to lead us. It will remind you that God is trustworthy.

3. Develop your gifts. Take classes. Gain information. Get counseling. Get more training and education. And practice, practice, practice. As your skills develop, you will have less fear of the future.

4. Lean on your support group. You need your support group to help comfort you in the changes you are going through. Lean on them, gain strength from them.

5. Learn from the witness of others. Get together with people who are struggling and have gone through what you have gone through. This is more than support. It is being able to hear the stories of people who have been there, who can witness to the fact that you can make it.

6. Have confidence in your ability to learn. Once you realize that you are able to learn new things and handle new situations, you cease fearing the future.

7. Rework past separations. Find someone with wisdom and begin to see if the fear and pain you are feeling as you face the present is coming from something unresolved in the past. This will help you get into perspective what you feel and perceive.

8. Structure. Internal structure will come from creating boundaries, but you may also need some strong external structure.

Set a certain time every day to call a friend, schedule weekly meeting times with your support group, or join a regular Bible study or a twelve-step support group. In chaotic times, you may need some structure around which to orient your new changes. As you grow, and the change is not overwhelming, you can begin to give up some structure.

9. Remember what God has done.
Remind yourself of what God has done and who he is.

Unforgiveness

Forgiveness means letting go of something that someone "owes" you. Gain grace from God, and let others' debts go. Do not keep seeking a bad account. Go and get what you need from God and people who can give. Unforgiveness destroys boundaries. Forgiveness creates them.

External Focus

You must confess the truth about the ways you are keeping your boundary-lessness going, and you must turn from those ways. You must look at yourself and face the internal resistance of wanting the problem to be on the outside of you.

Guilt

We have to be careful about listening to guilt feelings to tell us when we are wrong, for often, *the guilt feelings themselves are wrong*. Guilt distorts reality, gets us away from the truth, and away from doing what is best for the other person. Consider these guidelines:

1. Own the guilt.

2. Get into your support system.

3. Begin to examine where the guilt messages come from.

4. Become aware of your anger.

5. Forgive the controller.

6. Set boundaries in practice situations with your supportive friends, then gradually set them in more difficult situations.

7. Learn new information for your conscience. Learning God's ways can restore your soul and make your heart rejoice instead of feeling that controlling, parental guilt.

8. Acquire guilt. That may sound funny, but you are going to have to disobey your parental conscience to get well. You are going to have to do some things that are right but make you feel guilty. Do not let the guilt be your master any longer. Set the boundaries, and then get with your new supporters to let them help you with the guilt.

9. Stay in your support group. Guilt is not resolved by just retraining your mind. You need the new connections to internalize new voices in your head.

10. Do not be surprised by grief. This will be sad, but let others love you in that process. Mourners can be comforted.

Abandonment Fears: Taking a Stand in a Vacuum

Boundaries are not built in a vacuum. They must be undergirded by strong bonding to safe people, or they will fail. If you have a good support group to go to after setting boundaries with someone you love, you will not be alone.

If It Were Easy, You Would Have Done It By Now

These resistances will surely come.
See them in their biblical perspective.
They are part of a long history of
your sisters and brothers—people
who have encountered many trials as
they ventured out on the road of
faith, seeking a better land. This
journey is always riddled with trou-
ble, but also with the promises of
our Shepherd to carry us through if
we do our part. Go for it.

CHAPTER 15

HOW TO MEASURE SUCCESS WITH BOUNDARIES

Specific, orderly changes herald the emerging of mature boundaries. It's helpful to be aware of them. The following eleven steps allow you to measure your growth–to see where you are in your development.

Step #1: Resentment—
Our Early-Warning Signal

One of the first signs that you're beginning to develop boundaries is a sense of resentment, frustration, or anger at the subtle and not-so-subtle violations in your life.

Step #2: A Change of Tastes—
Becoming Drawn to Boundary-Lovers

As boundary-injured individuals begin developing their own boundaries, they become attracted to people who can hear their no without being critical. Without getting hurt.

Without personalizing it. Without running over their boundaries in a manipulative or controlling fashion.

Step #3: Joining the Family
As we find our tastes changing, we begin developing close and meaningful connections with people who have clear boundaries.

Step #4: Treasuring Our Treasures
After you feel safe being around people who believe that grace and truth are good (John 1:17), your values will start to change. You will begin to see

that taking responsibility for yourself is healthy, and you will begin to understand that taking responsibility for other adults is destructive.

Step #5: Practicing Baby No's

Growth in setting emotional boundaries must always be at a rate that takes into account your past injuries. Otherwise, you could fail massively before you have solid enough boundaries.

Step #6: Rejoicing in the Guilty Feelings

A sign that you're becoming a boundaried person is often a sense of self-condemnation, a sense that you've transgressed some important rules in your limit setting. That's why we encourage you to rejoice in the guilt. It means you are moving ahead.

Step #7: Practicing Grownup No's

Boundary setting is a large part of maturing. The goal is to have a character structure that has boundaries and that can set limits on self and others at the appropriate times.

Step #8: Rejoicing in the Absence of Guilty Feelings

You have changed from listening to your internal parent to responding to the biblical values of love, responsibility, and forgiveness. And these values have been internalized in the heart by many, many relational experiences with people who understand these values. The heart has somewhere to go for self-evaluation besides a critical conscience. The heart rests in the emotional memories of loving, truthful people.

Step #9: Loving the
Boundaries of Others

When we can love and respect the
boundaries of others, we accomplish
two things. First, we genuinely care
for another person. Second, we learn
empathy. It shows us that we need
to treat others as we would like to
be treated.

Step #10: Freeing
Our No and Our Yes

When you are as free to say no to
a request as you are to say yes, you

are well on the way to boundary maturity. There's no conflict, no second thoughts, no hesitation in using either word.

Step #11: Mature Boundaries— Value-Driven Goal Setting

Individuals with mature boundaries aren't frantic, in a hurry, or out of control. They have a direction in their lives, a steady moving toward their personal goals. They plan ahead.

The reward for their wise boundaries is the joy of desires fulfilled in life. Their investments in the years

God has given pay off for them.

It's our prayer that your biblical boundaries will lead you to a life of love, freedom, responsibility, and service.

NOTES

Chapter 3: Boundary Problems

1. An introduction to the four categories can be found in *Secrets of Your Family Tree*, by Dave Carder, Earl Henslin, John Townsend, Henry Cloud, and Alice Brawand (Chicago: Moody Press, 1991), 176–79.

Chapter 4: How
Boundaries Are Developed

2. The following structure was devloped
   by Margaret Mahler, and described in
   *The Pschological Birth of the Human
   Infant*, by Margaret Mahler, Fred Pine,
   and Anni Bergman (New York: Basic
   Books, 1975.) A researcher, Mahler
   observed the operationalizing of these
   biblical concepts in general revelation.

This book has been bound using handcraft methods and Smyth-sewn to ensure durability.

The dust jacket was illustrated by Michael McGovern.

The dust jacket was designed by John M. Lucas.

Text compiled from *Boundaries* by Henry Cloud and John Townsend, © 1992, Zondervan: Grand Rapids, MI.

The text was edited by Rebecca Currington in conjunction with Snapdragon Editorial Group, Inc.

The text was set in Baskerville Book.